CHARLESTON AND THE CAROLINA COAST

CHARLESTON
and the
CAROLINA COAST

Donato C. Rinaldi, Jr.

PALMETTO
PUBLISHING
Charleston, SC
www.PalmettoPublishing.com

Hardcover ISBN: 979-8-8229-2991-3
Paperback ISBN: 979-8-8229-2992-0
eBook ISBN: 979-8-8229-2993-7

CONTENTS

ACROSS THE GREAT ATLANTIC

Across the great Atlantic
A coastal jewel and crown
Inside her hidden harbor
A city Charles Towne

Beyond the eastern shoreline
A golden place was planned
A walled-in ancient city
Where holy steeples stand

The spires are your skyline
Above your city's lore
Beyond, the greatest nation
Atlantic at your door

The Ashley and the Cooper
Two rivers hand in hand
And just beyond the Wando
Creates a harbor grand

A city swells with promise
Atlantic treasured coast
Dealing with her history
She has her hidden ghosts

Her painted ladies standing
Below her Rainbow Row
Across the great Atlantic
Her harbor winds will blow

Through Civil War and scandal
Through prominence and shame
Through all those times, you're changing
Now, Charleston's your name

CHARLES TOWNE

Haunted streets I stumble down
Gnarly oaks of Charles Towne
Bending over ancient walks
Ivy covered letter box

Mansions old and standing tall
Iron gates and garden walls
Fountains trickle throughout time
Churches old and steeples chime

Spanish moss so softly swings
Onto trees the mosses cling
Gullah Geechie culture near
Sweetgrass baskets woven here

Lanterns lit to light the way
Gaslight flames burn years away
Narrow alleys without sun
Down the paths of Charleston

HOLY CITY HISTORY

Holy City's rising steeples
Packed with all the praying people
Rivers churning form her every shore

Walled in city was protection
Neighborhoods in every section
History behind each wooden door
Charleston is living evermore

Holy City's many stories
Shame to blame and many glories
Slavery into her soul it tore

The cobblestone and brick laid streets
Is where the past and present meets
History behind each wooden door
Charleston is living evermore

Holy City's alleys narrow
Far from pastures plowed and harrowed
Lace and satin that the ladies wore

Living in the upper classes
Silver spoons not shared by masses
History behind each wooden door
Charleston is living evermore

Holy City's taverns teaming
Summer streets are soaked and steaming
From a shower passing by her shore

Ghosts and goblins gayly peering
From the gardens so endearing
History behind each wooden door
Charleston is living evermore

Holy City's horse and carriage
Clopping down each narrow passage
Spilling secrets of forgotten lore

Lords of rice and kings of cotton
Someday may be long forgotten
History behind each wooden door
Charleston is living evermore

Holy City's future brightens
Spaces tighten. Numbers heighten
Popularity begins to soar

Visions of her future growing
People in her old homes knowing
History behind each wooden door
Charleston is living evermore

Holy City's neighbors present
John and James and ole Mount Pleasant
Many scenes and shorelines to adore

Blessed be your city shining
On your shoreline like a diamond
History behind each wooden door
Charleston is living evermore

SWEETGRASS BASKETS

Sweetgrass baskets made by hand
Hanging on a roadside stand
Fancy twists and ties I see
A part of southern history

Africa to Charleston
Where your basket weaving's done
Sweetgrass baskets filled with pride
More than mighty ocean tides

Sweetgrass baskets tell a tale
When the slave ships set a sail
Taken here against their will
Weaving sweetgrass baskets still

Gullah Geechie culture saved
With each basket southern made
Masterpiece of southern art
Every sweetgrass strand and part

Sweetgrass baskets woven tight
Hanging on a shanty site
Women twist and turn their art
Made with woven soul and heart

Beauty not just woven nice
Helping Gullah harvest rice
Holding this important tool
Sweetgrass baskets beauty, too

Sweetgrass baskets southern found
On the roads of Charlestowne
Many hundred years have passed
Sweetgrass Baskets made to last

CHARLESTON

Hydrangeas potted on the porch
Lanterns burning like a torch
Marshes dotted with wooden docks
Welcome flags on crooked walks

Piazzas sideways on the plot
Sumter sleeps while horses trot
Gardens rimmed with iron gates
Rainbow Row on East Bay waits

Gardenias bloom in iron urns
Front door porch's lantern burns
Carriage pulled through city streets
Clopping sounds from horse's feet

Petunia window boxes hang
Sunday choirs sweetly sang
Steeple bells in churches rung
Here I pray in Charleston

SINGING SONGS OF ANNALEE

Singing songs of Annalee
No other place I'd rather be
Pristine waters at her feet
Old world charm on every street

Singing songs of Annalee
Spanish moss in every tree
Islands off her eastern shore
Steeples in her city soar

Singing songs of Annalee
Crown of Carolina's sea
Grand piazzas paint her town
A jewel in Carolina's crown

Singing songs of Annalee
Crimson sunsets over thee
Under oaks for years you've grown
Annalee's my southern home

GATED GARDEN WALLS

Summer in the southern gardens
Northern breezes beg your pardon
Cooling winds are swirling down the lane

Over benches oak trees tower
Baskets filled with fragrant flowers
Like a chapter written by Mark Twain
Where the sweetgrass in the gardens reign

Pathways through the perfect plantings
Flowers on the stone wall granting
Passage passed the painted iron gate

Baskets with their flowers hanging
Screen door on the porch is banging
Gardens near the grist mill looking great
Colors painting porches evenings late

Fountains spilling, sweetly splashing
Tiny creatures dart and dashing
Watching as a flower petal falls

Sitting on a porch swing sleeping
Dreaming of the north winds sweeping
Cooling English ivy as it sprawls
Cobblestones and gated garden walls

STORMY DAY

Rolling down the wavy panes
Dripping to the sash
Raining on the farmer's grains
Hear the thunder crash

Peering from the windowsill
Dreary is the day
Cypress trees are standing still
Lightning lights the way

Shutters slam on cedar shakes
Windy is the storm
Evergreens for heaven's sake
Keep the cabin warm

Branches on the maple break
Falling to the lawn
Downpours filling up the lake
Where the water's drawn

Flooding shores where cabins sit
Branches float away
Pecan trees have bent a bit
On this stormy day

STEEPLES

Dark clouds rolling over me
The only lights that I could see
Steeples high near heavens kissed
Shining through the harbor's mist

Wooden boat was turned and tossed
Without the lights I would be lost
Steeples guide me to her shore
With my boat and broken oar

Thankful stepping on her land
Beneath the pointed lights I stand
Steeples led me to this place
By the will of my God's grace

Now, I lay me down to rest
My spirit here is surely blest
Steeples shined a light for me
When my soul was lost at sea

THE OLD WOODEN WRECK

Flags upon a wooden ship
Sitting in an ocean crypt
Currents wave them to and fro
In the water down below

Fish amazed by cotton flags
Creatures see the seaweed snags
Hauling nets the men would cast
Tangled in the broken mast

Sails were strewn on coral reefs
Creatures in their disbeliefs
Boxes, crates and paper bags
Strewn below the cotton flags

Both sides on the wooden ship
Gaping holes through something ripped
Cotton flags above the deck
Waving on the wooden wreck

Years on ocean floor it stood
Waterlogged and salty wood
As the starboard section sags
Currents wave the cotton flags

SILENCE BY THE LAKE

Silence by the lake
Not a ripple
Not a wake
Only surface gleaming glass
Tiger lilies and sour grass
The only movement floating by
Clouds reflecting from the sky
Not a movement in the trees
Not a wisping
Not a breeze
Peace is only what you make
Enjoying silence by the lake

CARRIAGE RIDES

Houses on your carriage rides
Porches running down the sides
Secret gardens no one sees
Chilling in the ocean breeze

Carriage rides on narrow streets
Colors on the houses, greet
Alleys long with branches low
East Bay blooms on Rainbow Row

Carriage rides near markets old
Many stories still untold
Only if these bricks could talk
On the streets where horses walk

Houses on your carriage rides
Stories past have come alive
Steeples ringing stories, too
Holy City, we love you

WOODEN WAGON WHEELS

Wooden wagon wheels on the cobblestone streets
Riding on the battery where all the rivers meet
Iron black cannons on the Cooper River shore
Spirits from the Ashley River haunt forevermore

Ladies on the battery greeting summers warm
Painted neighbors, like a rainbow, weather every storm
Gardens and gazebos are passed along the way
Horses pulling carriages that gallop near the bay

Thousands of her people in one hundred years have died
Neighbors and the spirits here are walking side by side
Steeples for three hundred years still dot her southern sky
Wooden wagon wheels on her streets still passing by

ANNALEE, OH ANNALEE

Annalee, oh Annalee
Your beauty full and spirit free
In your gown of cotton lace
A heart of gold and fair of face

Annalee, oh Annalee
The ocean washes over thee
With golden hair and salty kiss
Upon the beach I felt amiss

Annalee, oh Annalee
Your southern eyes have captured me
Passing through the city's lanes
A carriage led by horse's reins

Annalee, oh Annalee
Magnolia blooms on your tree
A fragrance fills the garden air
So happy that you met me there

Annalee, oh Annalee
A parasol to cover thee
Steeples standing side by side
Along your southern carriage ride

Annalee, oh Annalee
A fairer side I'll always see
Although I know your history
In my heart you'll always be

Annalee, oh Annalee
The carriage ride was hard on thee
Rest your weary head on me
Rest your weary head on me
Rest your head sweet Annalee

PARASOLS

With my vision keen and clear
I witnessed ghosts of yesteryear
High in collar donned with lace
Parasols to hide their face

Dresses long like royal gowns
Jewelry like golden crowns
Fingers painted rainbow bright
Parasols to block the light

Leather shoes strapped high on shins
Sachet bag to freshen sins
Steamer trunks for travel here
Parasols from yesteryear

With my vision clear and crisp
I witnessed ghosts appear as mist
In a flash the spirits gone
Parasols no longer donned

ANGELS

Angels on the streets of town
Roaming when the sun goes down
Corners under starry nights
Lanterns on the porches bright

Angels walk the city streets
Where the mighty rivers meet
Moonlight through the branches beam
Dancing on a water scene

Angels touch the evening sky
Starlight glistens in their eye
Strolling where the gardens meet
Battery and Meeting Street

Angels in the gardens sleep
Ripples in the Ashley sweep
Morning star, the harbor greets
Angels flee the city streets

Angels wait in heaven's plane
When evening's veil starts its reign
Quickly glimpse at starry nights
Angels on the porches bright

AN OLD CHARLESTON CEMETERY

The stones in rows like soldiers
Attention throughout time
The weather worn and withered
The stones in every line
The marble slabs were mighty
Some names too washed to read
The driving rain keeps falling
Attention's all they need

The stones in rows like soldiers
Beneath a canopy
The trees were worn and withered
The moss danced with the breeze
Some marble stones had fallen
Like soldiers in a field
The past for each keeps calling
In time their fate is sealed

CONFLUENCE AT CHARLESTON HARBOR

The waters rolled together
From north and east and west
They met at a confluence
Staying as a guest
Slowly moving onward
Into a churning sea
Returning never to
The place they used to be

The waters rolling forward
From shores they used to know
They met at a confluence
Mixing as they flow
Joining here, then onward
Into the great beyond
Returning never to
The place where they were fond

SEA ISLAND COTTON

A treasure from the sea and land
A precious gift from nature's hand
The purest white, this silky strand
Sea Island cotton once so grand

A fabric fit for royalty
and grown along King Charles' sea
It's best if worn for scones and tea
Sea Island cotton comforts me

A cotton worn by brides and grooms
You grace the finest noble looms
And cradle babes from mother's womb
Sea Island cotton picked and pruned

A fiber bringing coins of gold
The purest cotton ever sold
The softest fabric one can hold
Sea Island cotton story told

TOBACCO

Working in the fields
Where tobacco grows
Sticky fingers grasping
On my pappy's hoe
Digging soil here
On my family's land
Toil in my heart
And blisters on my hand

Working in the fields
Till my fingers bled
Turning earth in April
Planting every bed
Tending to the seedlings
Through the early days
Growing in the season
Under golden rays

Working in the fields
Where every seed is sown
Seedlings quickly growing
On my father's throne
Poor men have their riches
In the land they own
Daddy has a small shack
Our family calls it home

Working in the fields
On the humid days
Hundred-acre pasture
Under heavy haze
Soaking in my coveralls
Sweat on my brow
Two old beaten horses
Pulling pappy's plow

Working in the fields
In the summer sun
Mornings in the darkness
Till the day is done
Tying leaves in bundles
With my grandma's yarn
Hanging leaves we harvest
In tobacco barns

Working in the fields
Till the winter comes
Barely made a living
Stretching out the crumbs
April makes its presence
Planting once again
Toil in the fields
Till the season ends

MODERN DAY
CHARLES TOWNE

Haunted streets I stumble down
Changing times in Charles Towne
Thousands flocking to her shore
Changing tides and oceans roar

Crowded roads and alleys where
People meet her beauty there
Sandy beaches and waters warm
As she rides out every storm

Rivers wrap her ancient walls
Churches with their steeples tall
City market shows her fame
Artist's works and paintings framed

Fountains splash as children play
Rainbow Row cheers every day
Harbor breeze and southern sun
Forging paths in Charleston

DOUBLE DIAMONDS

Double diamonds rising high
In a southern summer sky
Spanning long across the bay
Greeting guests along the way

Seen for miles all around
No matter where or what your town
Dwarfing all the steeples high
In the Holy City's sky

Double diamonds in the night
With your facets shining bright
Dancing on the water low
On the skirt of city's glow

Standing strong without a sway
Reflecting diamonds on the bay
Serving as a guiding light
A beacon in the southern night

Double diamonds touching stars
In the evening near and far
From the islands on the sea
The grandest lighthouse guiding me

THE ANCIENT ASHLEY RIVER

Sweeping passed the gardens
Beneath the oaks so grand
The ancient Ashley River
Meanders through the land

Passing by in silence
Disturbing nothing green
A river hardly rolling
All through Low Country scenes

As she journeys onward
She grows in depth and breadth
Reaching Charles' City
Where no one there forgets

She's so greatly honored
For all the life she gives
The ancient Ashley River
Forever may she live

SAILBOATS ON THE ASHLEY

Sailboats on the Ashley
Seabirds flying free
Golden sun is rising
Summer on the sea
Schooners cut the waters
Fish are forced to flee
Swimming to the bottom
Where no wakes will be

Sailboats on the Ashley
Gliding through the glare
Atlantic breezes blowing
Gently through the air
Summer sun is standing
High above the sea
Shimmers on the surface
Dancing next to me

Sailboats on the Ashley
Sunshine in their sails
Pushed along the water
By the summer gales
Ashley meets the harbor
Longing to be free
Lost in the horizon
Sailing out to sea

Sailboats on the Ashley
Gliding fairly fast
Slicing through the water
Silent as they pass
Ocean breezes blowing
Strengths they can amass
Mainsail ropes are holding
Tightly on the mast

Sailboats on the Ashley
See the summer sun
Setting on the islands
When the day is done
James and John are waiting
Morris Island soon
Crimson sun is setting
For the southern moon

SAILBOATS ON THE ASHLEY
(Charleston Harbor)

Sailboats on the Ashley
Down the river's way
From the old plantations
Spilling in the bay
On her black tea water
Through her grand oak trees
Sailing the same rivers
With a different breeze

Sailboats on the Ashley
In her waters dark
Spanish Moss is hanging
Clinging to the bark
Winding through the lowland
Passing through with ease
As the river widens
Sailing out to sea

Sailboats on the Ashley
Cooper's on its way
Clashing in the harbor
All throughout the day
Cooper Ashley meeting
Mixing with the sea
Sailboats seem to gather
Where they like to be

Sailboats on the Ashley
Cooper River, too
With the Holy City
Perfectly in view
See her steeples standing
In the ocean breeze
Sailboats in her harbor
Slipping out to sea

BENEATH THIS TREE

And so, I stand beneath this tree
With limbs unfurling full and free
Fragrant flowers. Leaves of green
Spanish moss hangs in between
Sweetest sight I've ever seen

And so, I stand beneath this tree
It grows beside a raging sea
Stormy summers leave their mark
Standing stern through day and dark
Lovers names carved in the bark

And so, I stand beneath this tree
The girth is more than ten of me
Salty branches. Rugged roots
Owl at the treetop hoots
Creature through the soil scoots

And so, I stand beneath this tree
A beauty great and you'd agree
Timeless treasure. Ocean friend
Ancient sand on shorelines bend
Summer shade you always lend

And so, I stand beneath this tree
Our hands, we hold, just you and me
Ageless lovers. Countless days
Love unfurling where she stays
Cleansing us with ocean waves

And so, I stand beneath this tree
With limbs unfurling full and free
It grows beside a raging sea
Its girth is more than ten of me
A beauty great and you'd agree
Our hands, we hold, just you and me
The names we carved will always be
And so, I stand beneath this tree

A LIVE OAK'S BRANCHES KISS THE CREEK

A Live Oak's branches kiss the creek
And every day this scene repeats
A pleasant story now to share
About this beauty sweet and rare

A Live Oak tree was bending down
Its curving branches near the ground
It dipped across a wooden fence
That rambled on not making sense

The branches dipped down to a creek
Along a marsh where willows weep
The cotton clouds were dancing by
They're watching all the willows cry

The metal roofs on wooden docks
With heavy ropes and sailor's knots
Dot the marshes with grass so green
Along this pleasant summer scene

A Live Oak's branches kissed the waves
And with this kiss the water saves
The wakes were splashing on the shore
The willow trees will weep no more

The crooked fence just rambles on
The cotton clouds look down upon
A rolling creek with flying fish
This pleasant scene is all I wish

Across the creek, I saw that day
A heron slowly flies away
And every day this scene repeats
A Live Oak's branches kiss the creek

THE HORSE AND CARRIAGE

Somewhere here in Charleston
A carriage and a horse
Trotting down the narrow streets
But no one knows the source

On a corner, King and Broad
A breeze blows on my face
As if something passing by
But that was not the case

Hearing words of stories told
As if a carriage passed
Wheels turn on cobblestones
But never turning fast

Unknown echoes passing by
Along the Ashley coast
Horse and carriage don't appear
The driver is a ghost

SUMMERTIME IS ALMOST GONE

Picnic tables near a tree
Fluffy clouds above to see
Children playing on the lawn
Summertime is almost gone

Beaches blowing ocean sand
Lovers walking hand-in-hand
Waiting for another dawn
Summertime is almost gone

Early sunset on the waves
Moments of this summer saved
Windy palms and shaking prawns
Summertime is almost gone

Winter wind blows from the sea
Shaking every village tree
No one's playing on the lawn
Summertime was here and gone

HOW I LOVE MY ANNALEE

Maybe you can plainly see
How I love my Annalee
From her marshes salty sweet
To her shoreline's summer heat
Passed piazzas long and tall
City built inside a wall
Cradled by her harbor's hands
Sleeping in her salty sands

Maybe you can plainly see
How I love my Annalee
From her rivers spreading wide
To her horse and carriage ride
Passed her alleys paved with stone
Where her cotton once was grown
Standing in the harbor high
Gulls are gliding through her sky

Maybe you can plainly see
How I love my Annalee
From her markets on the street
To her people whom I meet
Passed the steepled holy place
Where I see her soul and face
Deep in lowlands you survive
Where your old oaks come alive

THE MARSH CAFÉ

Blue herons stood like statues
In marshes calmly waiting
For their morning breakfast
With nothing used for baiting

The egrets calmly watching
The ripples softly drifting
The mist has dampened feathers
The morning fog is lifting

The turtles float, then diving
The ripples onward flowing
Blue heron like a statue
His dampened feathers blowing

The egrets in the marshes
Enjoy this happy meeting
Until unfriendly fellow
A gator comes in greeting

The egrets and the herons
In marshes, they're not waiting
With gators there for breakfast
There is no use debating

CYPRESS ROOTS

Cypress roots with knobby knots
Blanketing my wooded lot
Forest filled with Cypress trees
Spreading all these knobby knees

Cypress roots with painful plans
Stubbing toes on scales so grand
Daily tripping hazard here
Walking forest lot in fear

Cypress roots are all around
Blanketing the forest ground
Once I fell on knobby knees
Spreading from the Cypress trees

Cypress roots not rooted deep
On the forest floor they creep
Spreading all those knobby knots
Surely, they're forget me nots

Cypress roots my mother said
Fall asleep on forest beds
Waiting for my knobby knees
Falling under Cypress trees

MAGNOLIA CEMETERY

There is a path we walk alone
Obelisks tall and granite stone
Those who have or have not sinned
Markers on the graves of men

There is a path we walk in time
You have yours and I have mine
Those who are or are not saved
Granite stones to mark their graves

There is a path we walk afraid
With chains we forged, daily made
Those who will or will not sin
Chains we wrought are carried in

There is a path I'm walking now
Tried to turn, but don't know how
Those who can or cannot try
No one here preferred to die

ELIZABETH ARDEN HOUSE

On a plot of gorgeous land
Here a home was built to stand
Against the tides and storms at will
The Arden House in Summerville

Iron fence and fancy gate
Ivy growing. Walks of slate
A diamond in the village crown
Her beauty like a bridal gown

Gardens flowing at her feet
Picturesque from Sumter Street
And with her trademark Arden door
Upon her steps it seems to soar

Crispy white where paths have led
Her long piazzas…Door of red
She stood for years through day and dark
As she's guarding Azalea Park

In her southern coastal state
Welcomes all into her gate
Gardens glow like a floral blouse
The Elizabeth Arden House

AS SURE AS TIDES
COME TWICE A DAY

As sure as tides come twice a day
I'll be here and gone away
Like a grain of southern sand
Washed into an ocean grand

As sure as tides come twice a day
Prints I leave will wash away
Like the leaves in mountain streams
Washed into a great ravine

As sure as tides come twice a day
Breath I take will blow away
Like the wind on prairies wide
Washed across the Great Divide

As sure as tides come twice a day
The summer sun will fade away
Like a candle melting quick
Washed away its dying wick

As sure as tides come twice a day
Birds will always fly away
Like the leaves in Autumn trees
Washed away by winter breeze

As sure as tides come twice a day
Snow will fall and melt away
Like the flakes from mountains come
Washed away by summer sun

ANNALEE, ANNALEE

Annalee, Annalee
She's acting from necessity
She's chained by her own history
Lost in what she used to be
Carries spirits in her soul
Freedom that her people stole
Facing new reality
My dearest, sweet love Annalee

Annalee, Annalee
She cradles her own destiny
A thriving city by the sea
Lost in her own revery
Dreaming all her dreams anew
Diversity is welcomed, too
Changing lady on the sea
My dearest, sweet love Annalee

Annalee, Annalee
She's working on her imagery
Architecture and artistry
Lost in her own tapestry
Strangers visit that she greets
Sandy beaches at her feet
Ocean lady on the sea
My dearest, sweet love Annalee

Annalee, Annalee
She raised her face in victory
Embracing her transparency
Lost in kind humanity
Spires soaring in her skies
Golden sunshine in her eyes
Grandest lady on the sea
My dearest, sweet love Annalee

OLD VILLAGE

On both sides of old Simmons Street
Is where the village comes to meet
Beside the harbor swift and deep
Is where this village sweetly sleeps

So many things to see and do
Along the streets to wander through
A peaceful walk in Pickett's Park
And Live oak trees with gnarly bark

Along your way the Pitt Street Bridge
Across the water just a smidge
Sullivan's shoreline softly waits
Beyond the mighty Moultrie gates

The village here took comfort in
Protection from the fortress then
She's resting now in peaceful place
With gnarly oaks and Spanish lace

The waters roll off Charleston
And glisten in the southern sun
They travel through the harbor's roar
The waves splash on the village shore

Across her green, Alhambra Hall
The cargo ships slow to a crawl
They're navigating toward the docks
The Cooper River rolls and rocks

A special place on Royall sits
The food will fill your soul with bliss
The sweetest shop is H and R
And old Shem Creek is not too far

And Hibben holds a secret Wreck
With screened-in porch and Shem Creek deck
So many more…to name a few
Old Mount Pleasant we all love you

A SUNFLOWER WEDDING
AT BOONE HALL

Sunflowers drooping their grand heavy heads
Wandering roots are buried in beds
Waiting for morning when glory will rise
Raising their faces up to the skies

Sunflowers lifting their grand heavy heads
Morning sun shining and warming their beds
Flowers are facing the sun's beaming rays
Daily this wedding at Boone Hall is praised

Sunflowers holding their grand heavy heads
Kissing the glory of sunshine from beds
Promise forever the flowers and sun
Another great day this wedding has done

Sunflowers searching with grand heavy heads
Evening is falling and cooling their beds
Searching the heavens for husbands they wed
Another grand wedding tomorrow it's said

Sunflowers drooping their grand heavy heads
Wandering roots still buried in beds
Waiting for morning when glory will rise
Weddings for flowers and sun in the skies

HURRICANE

Hurricane rain from the hurricane came
Across the Carolinas
The hurricane came
Raising up the ocean
Dancing with the pines
Soaking down the marshes
Shaking all the signs
Raging through the forests
Lashing in distain
Tearing through the village
Handing out its pain

Hurricane rain from the hurricane came
Across the Carolinas
The hurricane came
Driving through the daisies
Pounding in the parks
Racing up the rivers
Pushing through the dark
Crushing cotton fields
Losing many lives
Changing one's perspective
Finding who survives

Hurricane rain from the hurricane came
Across the Carolinas
The hurricane came
Blowing down the houses
Raking through the trees
Breaking through the windows
Raising up the seas
Dwelling over cities
Washing all the hope
Rising from the ashes
The Carolinas cope

THE SWINGING BAND

A breeze was blowing on the ocean air
A band was playing on the grandstand there
A man was dancing to the swinging songs
All this happened on the Isle of Palms

A wind was whirling on the sandy beach
A sun was setting on the outer reach
A kid was kicking all the snowy sand
A man still dancing to the swinging band

A child was clinging to the evening breeze
A wave was rolling from the southern seas
A bird was soaring in the setting sun
All this happened as the evening comes

A wind was whipping through the whirling palms
A moon was rising as the ocean calms
A man still dancing on the cooling sand
A last song playing by the swinging band

PLACED THE SUN WITHIN MY HAND

I stood upon the ocean's sand
I placed the sun within my hand
I raised my arms as sun did rise
And daylight filled the morning skies

The rays were bursting on the land
I placed the sun within my hand
My arms were straight above my crown
Until the sun was setting down

I watched on water, sunlight fanned
I placed the sun within my hand
My arms had settled by my sides
The sun beneath horizon, hides

SHADOW

As I walk along the beach
The sun behind me out of reach
Casting on the sandy shore
A shadow long and nothing more

As I walk, my shadow cast
Along the shoreline long and vast
Through my shadow on the shore
The waves are washing with a roar

Sweeping sand and salty sea
My shadow walks ahead of me
Through the seashells on the sand
Abiding with the passing land

Waves and shells and driftwood bleached
As long and far my shadow reached
Like a ghost through solid walls
My shadow passes through them all

Through the waves and seashells passed
As long as sun behind me lasts
My shadow gray will make its way
As I walk the beach today

CAROLINA CROOKED OAKS

Carolina crooked oaks
Along a path the river soaks
Serpentines a forest glen
Into a place it's never been

A hidden home it came across
Draped with clumps of Spanish moss
A window box of bright bouquets
Catching some of summer's rays

Carolina crispy leaves
Are swirling in a summer breeze
Lifting off the forest floor
They gather at a wooden door

The wooden door is weather worn
Silver splinters stick like thorns
Beside the window's bright bouquets
Spanish moss above it sways

Carolina crooked oaks
A river soaks these gnarly folks
Passed the forest's hidden home
Down an unknown path it roams

Remember all those crispy leaves
Blowing in the summer breeze
A few had hopped the river's ride
Escaping to the ocean's tide

Carolina coastal dreams
The hidden house is mine, it seems
Sitting near the wooden door
The Spanish moss drops to the floor

The forest air is smelling good
Hearth is filled with seasoned wood
Trees I felled keep fires stoked
Not a one from gnarly oaks

Carolina crooked oaks
The front porch swing is keeping notes
Autumn months and summer days
The river runs passed bright bouquets

The hidden house lies far behind
Ripples ride the waves of time
The river through my life it ran
Still the crooked oaks all stand

A PELICAN'S POEM

Are there poems for pelicans
The way they glide in flight
Or how they dive in raging seas
To taste a sweet delight

Are there poems for pelicans
The way they skim the shore
Or how they plunge into the seas
For tasty treats galore

Are there poems for pelicans
The way they like to stand
Or how they fly on distant seas
But always close to land

Are there poems for pelicans
The way I like to write
I wonder where these fellows go
As day turns into night

SULLIVAN'S ISLAND

Sullivan's, the place to meet
Maybe down on Middle Street
Share a pint with Edgar Poe
His tavern is a place to go

Sullivan's, the place to be
Underneath palmetto trees
In the breach, the Hunley crew
Sipped a pint of Edgar's brew

Sullivan's, is consummate
Has a daughter, Obstinate
She kissed the crew of Hunley men
Never to be seen again

Sullivan's, a place to love
Carolina sun above
Bordered on Atlantic sea
Sullivan's the place to be

PELICANS ON
SULLIVAN'S ISLAND

Pelicans piercing the sky like an arrow
Gliding the coast in a flock straight and narrow
Searching in sunshine that's beating on beaches
On Sullivan's Island's most outer reaches

With shovel in hand, I filled my old barrow
The whitest of sand like bleaching my marrow
I sat for a moment while thinking of leisure
I tend to this garden most purely for pleasure

Rows I have planted are all straight and narrow
With fountains and chimes and statues of pharaoh
I looked to the skies from my garden bench staring
My life is so good and no worse for the wearing

I continued the task of filling my barrow
Pelicans piercing the sky like an arrow
Though diving in oceans for dinner they're fishing
To land in my garden is all that I'm wishing

TO SEE THE SHORE

On my way to see the shore
Maybe live there evermore
Where the ocean meets the land
Where the beach has crystal sand

On my way to see the shore
Where the seagulls like to soar
Skimming on the ocean crest
Where they're feasting tastes the best

On my way to see the shore
With the dolphin pods galore
Where the waves of turquoise blue
Always different. Always new

On my way to see the shore
Just to dream and nothing more
Where the shoreline sand is fun
Underneath the summer sun

THE SHANTY BY THE SEA

The shanty by the sea
On a shoreline standing
Amazing sight to see
Where the ocean's landing
Along a grove of trees

The shanty by the sea
Near a village aging
Amazing sight to me
Where the ocean's raging
The waves are flowing free

The shanty by the sea
Where the church bells ringing
Amazing songs to Thee
Hear the songbirds singing
Within the blooming trees

The shanty by the sea
Where the palm trees swaying
Amazing ocean breeze
Where the shanty's staying
Beside the roaring seas

A MILLION RIPPLES

A million ripples rolling on
The surface that I see
Some are rolling far away
And some roll back to me
Each and every ripple has
A message I can keep
Underneath my pillow where
I lay my head to sleep

A million ripples rolling on
The surface of the sea
Each and every ripple has
A message left for me
Sometimes I can keep the message
Tucked with my dreams
Each and every ripple has
A different plan it seems

A million ripples rolling on
The surface soft and sweet
Some are rolling through my mind
And some roll passed my feet
I know it's hard to understand
What the ripples say
But I know their messages
Have helped me every day

SEA TURTLES

The storm was churning forcibly
Behind the turtle's path
The warmth of ocean waters
Now present her with its wrath
The waves were crashing endlessly
Near where I laid to rest
Turtles working hurriedly
To build their spawning nest

The breeze was blowing forcibly
Against the southern shore
The trees were bending gallantly
Above what tides had tore
My legs were stinging horribly
By pelting grains of sand
The eggs were buried seemingly
By turtles on the land

The eggs were breaking forcibly
Beneath a midnight moon
The trees were dancing gallantly
Above the sandy dune
The turtles hurried frantically
To reach the churning sea
Guided by the moonlight shining
It is their destiny

THOMSON PARK DUNES

There is a path through the dunes
To where the palm trees sway
Where I can see the ocean waves
Breaking on the bay

There is a sound when crashing waves
Hit upon the shore
The dunes are there to keep at bay
The mighty ocean's roar

There is a path through the dunes
To where the shoreline meets
And where the southern summer sun
Along the shoreline heats

Where once a church withstood a storm
Ending up in ruins
There is a town on coastal land
Protected by the dunes

There is a path through the dunes
That leads to ancient time
Where golden sun lights up the sky
On its morning climb

Soon the crimson ball will set
And paint the ocean skies
The passage through the dunes is dark
Away my spirit flies

BATTLE OF SULLIVAN'S
ISLAND 1776

There was a battle at the breach
The British tried to reach the beach
The cannon fire they'd soon abort
As cannon balls bounced off the fort

There was a battle at the breach
The inlet waters much too deep
The British thought they'd cross the bay
But all their forces turned away

There was a battle at the breach
The fort the British could not reach
The first attempt at Charles Towne
They almost brought the British down

There was a battle at the breach
Colonel Moultrie did not retreat
The British soon had scuttled boats
And turned away in their red coats

A TOAST TO EDGAR ALLAN POE

A secret Moultrie to we owe
A tale of Edgar Allan Poe
A tale of youth and thoughts be cursed
A tragic tale left unrehearsed

The tragic tales of Moultrie grow
The youth of Edgar Allan Poe
His army days on foreign lands
On Sullivan where Moultrie stands

A toast to Moultrie's raven soul
The life of Edgar Allan Poe
So blest we are for he was here
And still his ghostly breath be near

A toast to life. A toast to death
The ocean breeze. A raven's breath
A gift from Moultrie to we owe
A toast to Edgar Allan Poe

EDGAR, DEAR EDGAR

Edgar, dear Edgar
Your face is in the clouds
Looking down on Sullivan
Your tavern's awesome crowds
And just above the island
Gold Bug softly sleeps
Your soul within Fort Moultrie
Along the darkness creeps

Edgar, dear Edgar
Mount Pleasant to the west
Charleston in summertime
Will surely give her best
Atlantic slowly rising
Islands nevermore
Embrace the raven's message
And kiss my sweet Lenore

Edgar, dear Edgar
Please kiss my love goodbye
Still I see your face estranged
Along the southern sky
The ghost of you still haunts me
Your thoughts within me dwell
The story still unfolding
A tell tale heart to tell

A COZY COTTAGE ON THE COAST

A cozy cottage on the coast
Yesterdays are resting most
In its dusty, comfy chairs
Lives who've passed have spirits there

A hundred fifty years have passed
Shadows from the windows cast
In its wooden, paneled walls
Spirits from past summers call

An ocean crashing on the beach
Memories too far to reach
On its creaky, open porch
Lightning bugs die in the torch

A cozy cottage on the coast
Where I finally rest my ghost
On a fluffy, feathered bed
Where the spirits rest their heads

A hundred years will pass again
As another summer ends
Though the ocean waves still crash
Earth will turn my flesh to ash

SIPPING COFFEE

Sipping coffee by the sea
Feel its warmth inside of me
Deep within my soul to reach
Sipping coffee by the beach

Sipping coffee by the sea
Peaceful is this place to be
Warming mug cupped in my hand
Sipping coffee by the sand

Sipping coffee by the sea
On a bench beneath a tree
Soothing flavors bring me calm
Sipping coffee by the palm

Sipping coffee by the sea
Slowly finished, now empty
Cradled cup has not a drop
So, my sipping has to stop

PAPER DOLL
(A True Story from Sullivan's Island)

The lady asked for me to take her picture
In her hands, she held a paper doll
The ocean waves were crashing behind her
The tears on her cheeks began to fall

The lady hasn't seen this place in decades
In her heart was just an empty space
Her lover died and left her with no reason
They were supposed to meet in this place

The lady loved to listen to the ocean
He promised they would come here this Fall
Although he died beside her this past summer
In her hands she held a paper doll

You see, the paper doll was her dear lover
The only way that she could take him here
And after the picture of them was taken
The lady shed an ocean in each tear

SULLIVAN, OH SULLIVAN

Sullivan, oh Sullivan
Your beaches' beauty may
Slip into the oceanside
Or slide into the bay
Sitting on a sleepy fault
Your world may slip away

Sullivan, oh Sullivan
Your ocean crashing waves
Bashing into island homes
And washing into graves
Sitting on a sleepy fault
Destruction's all it craves

Sullivan, Oh Sullivan
Your sandy shoreline tossed
Crashing waves and rolling earth
Your beauty almost lost
Sitting on a sleepy fault
Your trust was surely crossed

Charleston, Oh Charleston
Your city's beauty dies
Fate depends strategically
On where this fault line lies
Sitting on a sleepy fault
Mount Pleasant surely cries

SULLIVAN'S ISLAND CHRISTMAS

Sullivan's Island Christmas
Your warm and salty air
Twists and turns on rooftops
Without a Christmas care

Sullivan's Island Christmas
Your warm and sandy beach
Twists and turns on shorelines
As far as eyes can reach

Sullivan's Island Christmas
Your warm and gentle breeze
Twists and turns on sand dunes
And through palmetto trees

Sullivan's Island Christmas
Your warm and wishful way
Twists and turns the heavens
Upon this Christmas Day

SEA CLOUD PLANTATION

Pluff mud walls with oyster shells
Marsh grass views and salty smells
Live oak trees in poignant patches
Shuttered glass and iron latches

Beehive well and broken bricks
Fallen oaks break stems and sticks
Old, stacked stones with mortar missing
Winds through Spanish moss is hissing

Icehouse stands so proud and white
Old house lost its former might
Sea Cloud ghosts through fields wander
Boneyard beaches over yonder

Nature claims this southern place
Where the Sea Cloud ghosts had grace
Live oak trees in poignant patches
Shuttered hearth and broken latches

THE BEACH AT BOTANY BAY

Spending time near gnarly oaks
Weathered by the salty sea
Strangers flock to see these folks
Haunting scene of these old trees

Roaming shores where dead trees stand
Branches stretch the water's ledge
Placing footprints in the sand
Strolling on the planet's edge

Nearing where each dead wood grips
Holding tight from washing waves
Many roots, the strangers grip
Gnarly oaks in silent graves

Seashells line the branches there
Beauty in this coastal scene
Never will you see, I swear
Beauty where there's nothing green

Seeing branches touched by death
Standing by the roaring seas
It will surely take your breath
Spending time near gnarly trees

ON THE SHORE OF
BOTANY BAY

There were seven live oaks standing
On the shore of Botany Bay
The boneyard bore their brothers
Where broken branches lay
Their bark was bleached from ocean salt
Left barren in the sand
The massive ghost-like monuments
Along the shoreline stand

There were seven live oaks weeping
On the shore of Botany Bay
The Spanish moss was dripping
The tears where brothers lay
The sea has reached the barren beach
Where dead oaks stand alone
But proudly, like a monument
Along their barren home

THUNDER AT PARADISE LANDING

The river echoed thunder
From clouds it's rolling under
The docks had their flags waving
A strike, the lightning craving

The forest watched in wonder
In fear of crashing thunder
The sound that it was making
The leaves on trees were shaking

The river echoed thunder
The birds, in nests, can't slumber
The fish are deeply swimming
The river's ripples skimming

The forest roots down under
Were hiding from the thunder
With all the trees not liking
The lightning bolts were striking

The river echoed thunder
From clouds it's rolling under
The flags on flag poles flying
A tree that's struck is dying

The world and all its wonder
The lightning and the thunder
For long it's never lasting
And so, this storm is passing

SLEEPING IN A SALTY MARSH

Sleeping in a salty marsh
The crashing waves I hear
Underneath the southern stars
I know the ocean's near

Underneath the midnight moon
The surface full and bright
Shining on the ocean near
Reflecting all her light

Glowing on the living oaks
The branches come alive
Knowing that her calming light
Is like my spirit guide

Sleeping in a salty marsh
The spirits of my past
Grasp my hand and surely guide
As long as life can last

LIVING OAKS IN
HIDDEN PLACES

The living oaks in hidden places
Shading all the happy faces
Dancing on the forest floor
Flowers, ferns and so much more

The living oaks in hidden places
Sharing all their given graces
Willing to protect the scenes
All around the forest green

The living oaks in hidden places
Spreading arms with Spanish laces
Reaching out in violent storms
Cradles creatures from all harm

The living oaks in hidden places
Wishing for a world it chases
Slipping through its canopy
Hidden for eternity

OLIVE SHELL

I found an olive shell today
As I shuffled on my way
This is how it came to be
When this olive greeted me

An olive shell from the sea
Rolled along in front of me
Tumbled sideways with the waves
Only one my spirit craves

Olive shell placed in my palm
Travelled from the ocean calm
Meets me here on southern sand
Placed the olive in my hand

Olive shell so smooth and round
Though not knowing where you're bound
In my palm is where you'll stay
I found an olive shell today

WILMINGTON HUES

Wilmington hues of crimson and red
Painting the sky around my ole head
Watching as waves are washing her shore
Giving some sand and stealing some more

Wilmington hues have brushed over blue
Evening approaching. Hours are few
Changing the canvas stretched on this scene
Watching the ocean shimmer with sheen

Wilmington hues that cover the sky
Setting the sun in marshes nearby
Raising the moon and stars in the night
Brightens the sand and gives it new light

Wilmington hues absorbed in the dark
Heavens are never missing their mark
Watching as waves are washing her shore
Stealing some sand and giving some more

NORTH AND SOUTH SANTEE

It's a very long bridge across the North Santee
Marsh grass and river water stretching to the sea
Georgetown far behind and so much in front of me
It's a very long bridge across the North Santee

Ancient waters follow paths down the river way
Old growth cypress standing tall where the osprey play
Gators on the muddy banks sunning for the day
Waters flowing through the marsh empty in the bay

It's another long bridge across the South Santee
Charleston County line is just in front of me
Georgetown far behind and the rivers flowing free
It's another long bridge across the South Santee

Ancient people living here fishing on the bank
Old growth cypress standing once, in the waters, sank
Gators on the muddy banks into waters yank
Unassuming feathered prey where it always drank

It's a very long bridge…The North and South Santee
Crossed those rivers many times crawling to the sea
Wishing that their ancient waters finally carry me
It's a very long bridge…The North and South Santee

HURRICANES AND HIGHER GROUND

Hurricanes and higher ground
Massive storm is shoreline bound
Radar watching for a while
Wider than three hundred miles

Searching for some higher ground
Storming ocean raging sound
Water waking over walls
Evacuation order calls

Ocean swelling in the bay
Flooding water feet away
Filling many bags of sand
Water rising on the land

People fleeing Battery
Houses boarded by the sea
Angry ocean, wicked skies
Leaving before someone dies

Hurricanes make history
Tragic scenes of misery
Praying this one doesn't though
Whether pressure's high or low

Hurricanes and higher ground
Evacuation of our town
Highways jammed with fleeing cars
Clouds won't let us see the stars

BOTTLE FROM THE SEA

I found a bottle floating in the southern sea
It bumped against my boat and damn it startled me
The winds were fiercely blowing, so I dropped my sail
I scooped the bottle up inside my metal pail

I pondered at this treasure holding in my hand
Who placed it in the ocean? Was it God or man?
The glass was worn and weathered from the churning sea
But I knew this treasure was only meant for me

I noticed in the bottle was a paper map
So my curiosity had me look at that
Words were written warning me, pointing to my fate
But I simply laughed it off. Raised my sail and weight

I quickly tossed the bottle back into the sea
As I sailed the violent storm bearing down on me
Snapping masts and tearing sails. Message could not wait
My broken boat washed ashore where I met my fate

CAROLINA COUNTRY STORE

Carolina Country Store
Coca-Cola and much more
Hershey bars and two cent gum
Children begging "Give me some."
Wooden floors that bend and creak
Locals go there every week
Mavis Jones and Grandpa Pete
Always where they like to meet
Sitting at the fountain bar
Neither has to walk too far
Reese's cups and Pixie Sticks
Tootsie Pops for many licks
Candy packed in old glass jars
M&M's and Mounds and Mars
All this stuff and so much more
Carolina Country Store

Carolina Country Store
Stephen Long and David Gore
Robyn James and brother Steve
Postman Gene will never leave
Even Dr. Alice stops
Selling all her homemade drops
Kevin Martin stops to eat
Sharon makes his life complete

Coffee beans the grinder mills
Dusty lights and dusty sills
B.C. powder. Goody's packs
Gasoline around the back
Walking on his merry way
Pastor Jim stops by each day
Keeping Bible near his chest
Making sure the folks are blest
All this stuff and so much more
Carolina Country Store

Carolina Country Store
Boiled peanuts by the door
Cornbread in a skillet baked
Sample pieces you can take
Chicken Bog on Monday night
Carmel cake's a sweet delight
Friday fish fry noon till five
"Customs" playing music LIVE
Danny dancing with a smile
Sue danced with him for a while
Joel, Teann and Joe stopped by
Victoria ate some apple pie
A jukebox filled with rock and roll
A guy named Elvis sang with soul
All this stuff and so much more
Carolina Country Store

Carolina Country Store
Sadly, they have closed their doors
Changing times and changing ways
Dreaming of the good ole days
Echoes at the fountain say
Mavis Jones has passed away
Empty jars where gum belongs
Grandpa Pete's been gone so long
Children once so young and bold
Children now have grown so old
Wooden floors with termite holes
Lollipops and Tootsie Rolls
Hershey bars no longer sold
Losing stories Grandpa told
Pastor Jim has joined the stars
Bible on the fountain bar
Coca-Cola sold no more
Carolina Country Store

A FUTURE BLEST FOR ANNALEE

Annalee, Oh Annalee
Your salty marshes meet the sea
Your harbors filled with billowed sails
From the ocean's summer gales

Annalee, Oh Annalee
Your bridges span the sky and sea
The waters bless your city's soul
Where your social changes flow

Annalee, Oh Annalee
Your alleys paved with history
And from a flawed and feral birth
Changing shows your city's worth

Annalee, Oh Annalee
Unfurled future in front of thee
And all your spirits laid to rest
Annalee your soul be blest

YOUNG STEPHEN'S
EAST BAY HOME

(In Honor and Loving Memory)

A mother
Her children
She's living life alone
A father
Two children
Young Stephen's East Bay home

A father
Two children
Three spirits heading west
A mother
Her children
And what no one had guessed

A mother
Her moment
Her older children grown
A father
His moment
Young Stephen's East Bay home

A father
Two children
With character that's best

A mother
In sorrow
So many children blest

A father
Two children
A fate that wasn't known
A mother
Her children
Young Stephen's East Bay home

A child
So, loving
Two brothers with their Dad
A mother
Her children
A sudden moment sad

A child
Young Stephen
A tragic tale he's known
A mother
He's helping
Young Stephen's East Bay home

This child
Was nurtured
A man into he's grown
His prestige
We honor
From Stephen Colbert's home

STARFISH

Starfish on a Christmas beach
Seashells scattered within reach
Ocean waves December morn
On this day that Christ was born

Starfish tops a Christmas tree
Ocean waves roll from the sea
From the Book this word was sworn
On this day that Christ was born

Starfish stern in Christmas breeze
Where shorelines sitting never freeze
Charleston, your faith unworn
On this day that Christ was born

Starfish seen in Christmas night
Shining on the shells so bright
Shoreline beaches toasty warm
On this day that Christ was born

Starfish shoots through Christmas sky
High above where angels fly
Charleston, your grace adorns
On this day that Christ was born

A CHARLESTON SNOWFALL

The stores were tightly packed
The bricks were old and stacked
The doors were wood and worn
The bells would ring each morn

The streets were cobblestone
The flags were proudly sewn
They hung from second floors
They topped the wooden doors

The glass in windows waved
From years the windows aged
The frost on windows formed
The sills had plants adorned

The posts in alleys bright
The streets were snowy white
The folks walked cobblestones
To shops with tea and scones

They reached the stores at last
The time through doors had passed
The walls where bricks were stacked
Though some had worn and cracked

As long as time could tell
The town and stores were well
The doors and handles worn
They open every morn

The sounds of songs were sung
The bells in churches rung
The snow on steeples fell
And then, it bid farewell

SOUTHERN WINTER WONDERLAND

The ocean air is crisp as leaves
Falling from November trees
The beach is cool upon my feet
Where winter wind blows beneath
Pretending crashing waves are snow
As the blankets ebb and flow
The seafoam castles on the sand
Stretch across my wonderland

The ocean air is crisp and clean
Blowing on my winter scene
The beach below my feet is cool
Northern winds can be so cruel
Blowing across the southern shore
Waves are crashing with a roar
The seafoam looks like snow on sand
Southern winter wonderland

CAROLINA CHRISTMAS DAY

Carolina Christmas Day
Warm and sunny on its way
Seashells on the Christmas tree
Here is where I wish to be

Carolina Christmas Day
Watching as the palm trees sway
Painted seashells done by hand
Seagulls resting in the sand

Carolina Christmas Day
Ocean treasures on display
Starfish top the Christmas trees
Wreaths of oyster shells to see

Carolina Christmas Day
Sun shines peace through every ray
Strolling beaches hand-in-hand
Christmas trees drawn in the sand

Carolina Christmas Day
Once I heard the summer say
Winter's blessed with warmth and sun
Pleasant days for everyone

Carolina Christmas Day
Where I hear the children say

"Let's ride our surf boards like a sleigh
Down the sand dunes here today."

Carolina Christmas Day
How the children love to play
Stockings filled with candy canes
Seeing Santa pull the reins

Carolina Christmas Day
Peace on earth is all I pray
Comfort in the ocean waves
As my spirit soul He saves

Carolina Christmas Day
On your beaches where I lay
Painted seashells all around
This is where my soul is found

Carolina Christmas Day
Summer breezes on the way
Seashells painted with delight
Thank you for this Christmas sight

Carolina Christmas Day
Santa rests here with his sleigh
On a beach of ocean blue
Carolina, I love you.

CHARLESTON CHRISTMAS

Christmas carols, Charleston
With gentle voices, southern sung
Along the bay near Rainbow Row
The salty air is Christmas snow

Christmas carols, Charleston
Are heard from where the stockings hung
Along your streets of cobblestone
A fire burns in every home

Christmas carols, Charleston
Among your steeples, holy one
The Battery holds back the storm
We have your hearth to keep us warm

Christmas carols, Charleston
In gentle voices, southern sung
No matter where your soul is from
Your heart will stay in Charleston